The Magic Pomegranate

A Jewish
Folktale

By

Peninnah Schram

Illustrated by

Melanie Hall

M Millbrook Press/Minneapolis

This story is adapted from "The Magic Pomegranate" in Peninnah Schram's *Jewish Stories One Generation Tells Another*, first published in 1987 by Jason Aronson, an imprint of Rowman & Littlefield Publishers, Inc., Lanham, MD.

Millbrook Press
A division of Lerner Publishing Group, Inc.
241 First Avenue North
Minneapolis, MN 55401 USA

For reading levels and more information, look up this title at www.lernerbooks.com.

Library of Congress Cataloging-in-Publication Data

Schram, Peninnah.
    The magic pomegranate / retold by Peninnah Schram ; illustrated by Melanie Hall.
        p. cm. — (On my own folklore)
    Summary: Three handsome and clever brothers compete to find the world's most unusual gift. Includes a note on doing good deeds, or mitzvah, and discusses the symbolism of the pomegranate in Judaism.
    ISBN 978-0-8225-6742-4 (lib. bdg. : alk. paper)
    ISBN 978-1-58013-657-0 (eb pdf)
    [1. Fairy tales. 2. Pomegranate—Folklore. 3. Jews—Folklore.] I. Hall, Melanie W., ill. II. Title.
    PZ8.S3118Mag 2008
    398.2—dc22 [E]   2006036722

Manufactured in the United States of America
7-43076-5552-10/4/2016

to Dorielle, Aaron, and Ilan—who love pomegranates
—P.S.

to the memory of Fred Brenner, my dear teacher
at Marywood University
—M.H.

Once, very long ago,
there were three brothers
who loved adventure.
One day, they decided to go on a journey,
each one to a different country.
They agreed to meet again 10 years later.
Each brother was to bring back
an unusual gift.

The oldest brother decided
to go to the west.
When he arrived
in a certain town,
he saw many fascinating things.
Magicians, dancers,
jugglers, and acrobats—
marvelous sights whirled
all around him.

As the brother watched the entertainments, he saw one magician hold up a magic glass. Through the glass, the magician could see the most distant corners of the kingdom.

"Ah!" thought the oldest brother.
"I would like to have that glass.
It would certainly be an unusual
object to share with my brothers."
He asked the magician,
"Tell me, how much is that glass?
I should like to buy it from you."

8

At first, the magician
would not part with his magic glass.
But after much pleading by the brother
and much bargaining by the magician,
they agreed upon a price.
The glass now belonged
to the oldest brother.

The second brother
traveled to a country in the east.
Wherever he went,
he kept his eyes open—
and his mind as well.
He was always looking
for the most unusual gift
that he could bring back
to his brothers.

One day, he heard drum beats
coming from the shop
of an old carpet seller.
They drew him to the store.
The seller called out,
"Carpets for sale!
Beautiful, wonderful carpets here!"

The brother stopped
to examine the seller's goods.
Suddenly, he saw one carpet
at the bottom of the pile begin to move.
It seemed to be moving by itself!
"What kind of carpet
is this one?" he asked,
pointing to the bottom one.

12

The old merchant motioned
for the brother to bend down.
He whispered in his ear,
"This is a *magic* carpet.
Buy it, and it will take you
anywhere you want to go—and quickly too!"
So the second brother
bargained with the carpet seller
until they settled upon a price.
The brother left with the magic carpet,
satisfied that he had a most unusual gift.

The youngest brother
went to the south.
He traveled far and wide
through the countryside.
He searched for something special
to bring back to his brothers.
This country in the south
had many lush and famous forests.

One day, the youngest
brother came upon a
grove of trees.
All at once,
he noticed
something strange.

One tree in the grove was a different shape
than the hundreds of other trees around it.
It was a pomegranate tree,
covered with orange red blossoms.
It was the most beautiful tree
that he had ever seen!
But as the youngest brother came closer,
he saw that the tree had only one pomegranate.
"This is strange indeed,"
thought the young man.
"A pomegranate tree
with only one pomegranate."
He approached the tree slowly.
He laughed to himself as he thought of
the story he would tell his brothers
about the pomegranate tree
with many blossoms
but only one fruit.

Full of wonder,
the youngest brother
reached for the beautiful pomegranate.
The fruit fell into his hand
even before he could pluck it
from the branch.
At that very moment, another pomegranate
burst from one of the blossoms.
The youngest brother looked down
at the pomegranate in his hand.
He said to himself,
"This must be a magic pomegranate.
But what magic does it perform, I wonder?"

The youngest brother
gazed at the pomegranate.
He marveled at its beauty.
"Its shape is perfect," he thought,
"crowned with the crown of King Solomon."
He walked away from the tree slowly,
still looking at his mysterious, new treasure.

Before he left the grove, he looked back
to see the pomegranate tree once more.
But the tree had vanished.
"Now I know this is a magic pomegranate,"
the youngest brother thought.
"And so this is what I will bring
to my brothers."

Ten years passed.

When the three brothers

met as they had planned,

they embraced with delight.

Eagerly, they showed one another

the unusual objects

they had brought back from their journeys.

The oldest brother said,

"Let me look through my glass

and see what I can see."

But when he held up the glass,

he saw a troubling scene.

In a far-off kingdom,

a young princess lay ill, near death.

"Brothers!" the oldest brother cried.

"We must help her!"

"Quickly, dear brothers,"
said the second brother.
"Get on my magic carpet,
and we will fly there!"

In what seemed like seconds,
the three brothers arrived
in the far-off kingdom.

In the royal palace of the kingdom,
the king was grief stricken.
He had sent for every doctor in the country
to cure his daughter,
but they had all failed.
It seemed there was no hope
left for the princess.

The king finally sent a messenger
throughout the country.
The messenger carried the king's words:
"Whoever can save my daughter,
the princess,
will have her hand in marriage
and half the kingdom!"

As if in a dream,
the youngest brother
heard a voice whisper inside him.
"The pomegranate!" it urged.
"The magic pomegranate!"

The youngest brother stepped forward.

He asked the king,

"May I try to cure the princess?"

Desperate with grief, the king agreed.

He led the young man to the princess's chambers.

In her room, the princess lay
deathly ill on her bed.
She was beautiful but pale with sickness.
The youngest brother approached quietly.
He sat down by her side.
Then he took the pomegranate from his pocket.
He cut it open with gentle care,
carving each juicy seed from its place.
He fed the rich red kernels to the princess,
one by one.

In a few moments,

the princess felt stronger.

The color returned to her cheeks.

Soon she sat up in her bed,

fully restored to health.

The king was overjoyed.

He hugged his daughter tightly.

Turning to the three young men, he said,

"The man who saved my daughter

will marry her."

The three brothers began to quarrel.

Each claimed to be the one

who should marry the princess.

The oldest brother said,

"If it were not for my magic glass,

we would never have known

that the princess was ill.

I deserve to marry the princess."

"But, brothers,
it was because of my magic carpet
that we could arrive so quickly,"
argued the second brother.
"Otherwise, the princess
would surely have died.
I deserve to marry the princess."

Finally, the youngest brother said quietly,
"It was my magic pomegranate
that healed the princess.
I deserve to marry the princess."

The three brothers could not agree
on which one of them
should marry the princess.
So the king tried to decide.
He looked at the three young men.
He looked from one to the next
and then the next.
Each was clever. Each was handsome.

The king could not decide

who deserved to marry his daughter.

At last, the king turned to the princess.

She was as wise as she was beautiful.

He asked her,

"Knowing you are wise, my daughter, tell me.

Who do you think deserves to marry you?"

The princess answered simply,
"I will ask each of them a question."
She turned to the oldest brother and asked,
"Has your magic glass changed in any way
since you arrived in this kingdom?"
"No," answered the oldest brother.
"My glass is the same as always.
I can look through it and see
to every corner of this kingdom."

Then the princess looked
at the second brother.
"Has your magic carpet changed in any way
since you arrived in this kingdom?"
she asked.
And the second brother answered,
"No, my carpet is the same.
I can fly anywhere on it, as always."

Finally, the princess turned
to the youngest brother.
She asked,
"Has your magic pomegranate changed
in any way
since you arrived in this kingdom?"

And the youngest brother answered,
"Yes, princess.
My magic pomegranate is no longer whole,
for I gave you part of it."

The princess then turned
to all three young men.
She announced her decision.
"I will marry the youngest brother,"
she said.
"It is he who performed
the greatest good deed,
because he gave up something of his own."

The brothers and the king
understood the wisdom of the princess.
The youngest brother had given most freely,
most selflessly.
So the reward that he earned
was the most treasured.

The king was delighted.
The other two brothers
nodded in agreement.
The princess and the youngest brother
were married in a beautiful wedding.

Then the king said,
"From this time on, I appoint
the three brothers and the princess
to serve as my royal advisers."
And so it was!

Author's Note

The Magic Pomegranate is one of my favorite stories to tell. It's called a cumulative tale. That means that several people contribute to the solution of the problem. In this case, the problem is how to cure the princess.

People all over the world tell this type of folktale. This specific story is uniquely Jewish because it draws on an important lesson from the Talmud (a sacred text of Jewish teachings and of commentaries on the Jewish Bible). That lesson is that the greatest mitzvah (good deed) is performed by the person who gives of himself or herself or who gives up something of his or her own.

There are many versions of this story in Jewish folklore throughout the Middle East and Eastern Europe. Often a magic apple or potion is used to cure the princess. I have changed the healing element to the marvelous pomegranate. To me, the pomegranate is truly a magical fruit that has a great deal of symbolism in Judaism. According to Jewish tradition, a pomegranate has 613 juicy kernels—one for each of the 613 mitzvoth (good deeds) that a Jew should perform. The fruit is mentioned in the Bible, which is known as the Torah in Hebrew. The pomegranate is called one of the seven choice fruits of Israel. I especially love the saying from *Song of Songs Rabba* (6:11): "Children, sitting in a row studying Torah, are compared to the compact kernels of a pomegranate."

Glossary

King Solomon: Solomon lived in the tenth century B.C.E. and became the third king of Israel. As a folktale hero, he is famous for his wisdom. According to legend, King Solomon's crown was made in the shape of a pomegranate crown.

pomegranate: the name of this fruit comes from the Latin *pomum granatum*. These words mean "apple having many seeds." Or the name may come from the Middle French *pome garnete*, which means "seeded apple." The pomegranate is sometimes called a Chinese apple.

Talmud: the commentaries on the Torah that were passed down through the generations. The Talmud is a great storehouse of Jewish history and customs. It combines law (*halakha*) and lore (*ugada*). It is the most sacred Jewish text after the Torah.

Torah: the Jewish Bible

Further Reading

Oberman, Sheldon. *Solomon and the Ant and Other Jewish Folktales.* Honesdale, PA: Boyds Mills Press, 2006. This collection of 43 Jewish folktales includes religious, wisdom, riddle, and trickster tales.

Schram, Peninnah. *The Hungry Clothes and Other Jewish Folktales.* New York: Sterling Publishing Co., Inc., 2008. These 22 folktales from Ashkenazi and Sephardic oral traditions focus on wisdom, wit and clever reasoning to bring about a just resolution.

Schram, Peninnah. *Jewish Stories One Generation Tells Another.* Lanham, MD: Jason Aronson, an imprint of Rowman and Littlefield Publishers, Inc., 1987. These 64 stories come from various Jewish oral and written traditions. They include Elijah the Prophet tales, King Solomon legends, and a wide variety of folktales.

Schwartz, Howard *The Day the Rabbi Disappeared: Jewish Holiday Tales of Magic.* Phildadelphia: Jewish Publication Society, 2003. This book presents a story for each of 12 important holidays. The stories feature magical feats performed by a wise rabbi for the benefit of the Jewish people.